MAD LIBS JUNIOR

ANIMALS, ANIMALS, ANIMALS!
MAD LIBS JUNIOR

By Roger Price and Leonard Stern

Mad Libs
An Imprint of Penguin Random House

MAD LIBS
Penguin Young Readers Group
An Imprint of Penguin Random House LLC

Concept created by Roger Price & Leonard Stern

Published by Mad Libs,
an imprint of Penguin Random House LLC,
345 Hudson Street, New York, New York 10014.
Printed in the USA.

ISBN 9780843109511
17 19 20 18

MAD LIBS ☺ JUNIOR.
INSTRUCTIONS

MAD LIBS JUNIOR™ is a game for kids who don't like games!
It can be played by one, two, three, four, or forty.

RIDICULOUSLY SIMPLE DIRECTIONS:

At the top of each page in this book, you will find four columns of words, each headed by a symbol. Each symbol represents a part of speech. The symbols are:

★	☺	→	?
NOUNS	ADJECTIVES	VERBS	MISC.

MAD LIBS JUNIOR™ is fun to play with friends, but you can also play it by yourself! To begin, look at the story on the page below. When you come to a blank space in the story, look at the symbol that appears underneath. Then find the same symbol on this page and pick a word that appears below the symbol. Put that word in the blank space, and cross out the word, so you don't use it again. Continue doing this throughout the story until you've filled in all the spaces. Finally, read your story aloud and laugh!

EXAMPLE:

"Good-bye!" he said, as he jumped into his _____ and _____
                                                    ★   →

off with his pet _____ .
                         ?

★	☺	→	?
NOUNS	ADJECTIVES	VERBS	MISC.
car	curly	drove	hamster
boat	purple	~~danced~~	dog
roller skate	wet	drank	cat
taxicab	tired	twirled	~~giraffe~~
~~surfboard~~	silly	swam	monkey

"Good-bye!" he said, as he jumped into his __SURFBOARD__ and __DANCED__
                                                    ★   →

off with his pet __GIRAFFE__ .
                         ?

In case you haven't learned about the parts of speech yet, here is a quick lesson:

A **NOUN** ✦ is the name of a person, place, or thing. *Sidewalk, umbrella, bathtub,* and *roller blades* are nouns.

An **ADJECTIVE** ⊚ describes a person, place, or thing. *Lumpy, soft, ugly, messy,* and *short* are adjectives.

A **VERB** ➔ is an action word. *Run, jump,* and *swim* are verbs.

MISC. ? can be any word at all. Some examples of a word that could be miscellaneous are: *nose, monkey, five,* and *blue.*

MAD LIBS JUNIOR™ is fun to play with friends, but you can also play it by yourself! To begin, look at the story on the page below. When you come to a blank space in the story, look at the symbol that appears underneath. Then find the same symbol on this page and pick a word that appears below the symbol. Put that word in the blank space, and cross out the word, so you don't use it again. Continue doing this throughout the story until you've filled in all the spaces. Finally, read your story aloud and laugh!

A _____ FOLLOWED ME HOME
?

★ NOUNS	😀 ADJECTIVES	➡ VERBS	? MISC.
nest	weird	bark	giraffe
tree	shiny	scream	ladybug
car	boring	dance	hippo
haystack	crazy	wiggle	rabbit
bush	fuzzy	jump	dinosaur
cake	fun	waddle	worm
puddle	silly	skip	goldfish
hole	goofy	laugh	monkey
hat	smelly	screech	snake
truck	slimy	bounce	horse
tree house	hairy	sing	tiger
airplane	stinky	growl	penguin

MAD LIBS JUNIOR

A _____ FOLLOWED ME HOME
?

I had just left my _____ piano lesson and was walking home

when a giant _____ jumped out of a/an _____. It
? ★

was as big as a _____ and it started to _____.
? ➡

Wow! What a _____ _____! I started to walk
?

home and it began to _____ as it followed right behind me.
➡

When I got home, my mom started to _____ and said, "Where
➡

did you get that _____ creature?!" "He followed me home," I

said. "I think he'd make a really _____ pet. Can I keep him,

please?" Can you believe she said yes? Now he sleeps in a big

_____ in my backyard and we do everything together!
★

MAD LIBS JUNIOR™ is fun to play with friends, but you can also play it by yourself! To begin, look at the story on the page below. When you come to a blank space in the story, look at the symbol that appears underneath. Then find the same symbol on this page and pick a word that appears below the symbol. Put that word in the blank space, and cross out the word, so you don't use it again. Continue doing this throughout the story until you've filled in all the spaces. Finally, read your story aloud and laugh!

DOG SHOW

★ NOUNS	☺ ADJECTIVES	➡ VERBS	? MISC.
cupcake	tiniest	bark	poodle
hot dog	best	bounce	cocker spaniel
cream puff	worst	shake	bulldog
pumpkin	funniest	roll	wolfhound
taco	smelliest	dance	sheepdog
sausage	smallest	jump	collie
hamburger	cutest	laugh	Great Dane
cookie	smartest	smile	pit bull
pretzel	coolest	sneeze	greyhound
pepper	silliest	sing	dalmatian
steak	craziest	juggle	beagle
meatloaf	wildest	clap	mutt

MAD LIBS JUNIOR

DOG SHOW

Every year, the Keystone Kennel Club hosts a dog show to find

the _____ dog in the world. This year, I entered my

_____, "_____." I've trained her to

_____ and to _____ on command. Every time she

does a trick right, I feed her a _____. At the dog show, she ran

out in front of the judges and started to _____. The crowd

went wild and a big _____ behind her started to

_____. She didn't win the big prize, but was awarded the

prize for _____ in Show. We won a huge trophy shaped like a

_____. I can't wait for the dog show next year!

MAD LIBS JUNIOR™ is fun to play with friends, but you can also play it by yourself! To begin, look at the story on the page below. When you come to a blank space in the story, look at the symbol that appears underneath. Then find the same symbol on this page and pick a word that appears below the symbol. Put that word in the blank space, and cross out the word, so you don't use it again. Continue doing this throughout the story until you've filled in all the spaces. Finally, read your story aloud and laugh!

BUG HUNT

★	☺	→	?
NOUNS	**ADJECTIVES**	**VERBS**	**MISC.**
net	smelly	cry	snails
hat	slimy	yell	spiders
mug	gross	run	butterflies
toilet	nasty	jump	beetles
bucket	weird	sing	ladybugs
jar	funny	fly	fireflies
cup	shiny	dance	crickets
briefcase	cool	snort	centipedes
sock	scary	screech	moths
backpack	neat	clap	ants
trash can	sweet	sneeze	bees
lunch box	crazy	shake	fleas

MAD LIBS ☺ JUNIOR™
BUG HUNT

My friend Sara and I love to look for _____ bugs in the park ☺

in the summertime. When we go on a bug hunt, we always take a

_____ ★ to put the bugs we find in. I like to look for

_____ ★ ?, but Sara likes _____ ? the best. One time we

even found some purple _____ ? squirming around under an

old _____ ★. I think bugs are really _____ ☺. Did you

know that some _____ ? can _____ ➡ just like

people? My dad thinks _____ ? are _____ ☺. One time

I caught one on a bug hunt and put it in his _____ ★. When he

saw it, he started to _____ ➡. I laughed so hard, I started to

_____ ➡!

MAD LIBS JUNIOR™ is fun to play with friends, but you can also play it by yourself! To begin, look at the story on the page below. When you come to a blank space in the story, look at the symbol that appears underneath. Then find the same symbol on this page and pick a word that appears below the symbol. Put that word in the blank space, and cross out the word, so you don't use it again. Continue doing this throughout the story until you've filled in all the spaces. Finally, read your story aloud and laugh!

ALLERGIC TO CATS

★	☺	➜	?
NOUNS	**ADJECTIVES**	**VERBS**	**MISC.**
face	itchy	cry	hippo
sleeping bag	slimy	sneeze	dinosaur
shirt	smelly	cough	cow
foot	squishy	laugh	moose
toothbrush	nasty	dance	elephant
bag	puffy	shake	pig
towel	stinky	choke	horse
slipper	furry	sing	gorilla
head	shiny	wheeze	whale
tummy	soft	melt	blowfish
suitcase	gross	snort	rhinoceros
arm	hairy	itch	octopus

MAD LIBS JUNIOR
ALLERGIC TO CATS

I'm so allergic to cats that if I come within ten feet of one, I start to

_____. Then I swell up to the size of a/an_____.

My skin breaks out in red, _____ bumps and I begin to

_____. One time I spent the night at my _____

friend Dave's house. In the middle of the night, his cat came and slept on

my _____. When I woke up, my throat was swollen and I felt

like I'd swallowed a/an _____. My _____ was so

_____ that I had to go to the hospital and get a shot. The only

good thing about being allergic to cats is that I get to have a pet

_____ instead!

MAD LIBS JUNIOR™ is fun to play with friends, but you can also play it by yourself! To begin, look at the story on the page below. When you come to a blank space in the story, look at the symbol that appears underneath. Then find the same symbol on this page and pick a word that appears below the symbol. Put that word in the blank space, and cross out the word, so you don't use it again. Continue doing this throughout the story until you've filled in all the spaces. Finally, read your story aloud and laugh!

SUMMER SAFARI

★	😊	➡	?
NOUNS	**ADJECTIVES**	**VERBS**	**MISC.**
camera	wild	barking	yak
pickle	crazy	yelling	jellyfish
candy bar	scary	sneezing	worm
guitar	bumpy	growling	snail
banana	nasty	talking	gerbil
hot dog	fuzzy	eating	kitten
toilet	smelly	dancing	donkey
sandwich	cool	singing	zebra
waffle	furry	crying	bunny
pizza	weird	smiling	warthog
coconut	goofy	laughing	squid
stick	hairy	swimming	guinea pig

Last summer, my family went on safari to Africa to spot a

_____ _____ . A safari is like a _____

camping trip where, if you're lucky, you will see a _____ .

The whole time, my dad wore a really _____ hat and

carried a _____ with him everywhere he went. He got really

excited when we saw a _____ _____ at a watering

hole. Another time, a wild _____ started _____

and charged at our safari van. It finally left us alone when my mom began

_____ like a _____ and dropped a

_____ out of the van window. My favorite thing to see on

safari was a mother _____ and her babies eating a

_____ .

MAD LIBS JUNIOR™ is fun to play with friends, but you can also play it by yourself! To begin, look at the story on the page below. When you come to a blank space in the story, look at the symbol that appears underneath. Then find the same symbol on this page and pick a word that appears below the symbol. Put that word in the blank space, and cross out the word, so you don't use it again. Continue doing this throughout the story until you've filled in all the spaces. Finally, read your story aloud and laugh!

HOW TO CATCH A WILD _____

?

★ NOUNS	☺ ADJECTIVES	→ VERBS	? MISC.
toothpicks	sturdy	kick	squirrel
oranges	hairy	bite	penguin
sardines	bumpy	squeeze	dolphin
peanuts	tough	chuckle	camel
chicken wings	spiky	lick	elephant
potato chips	crunchy	smell	boar
noodles	hard	pinch	poodle
jelly beans	furry	kiss	mouse
pancakes	squishy	sniff	goat
onions	tasty	hug	alligator
socks	crispy	poke	lobster
gum balls	floppy	whack	chickadee

MAD LIBS JUNIOR

HOW TO CATCH A WILD _____ ?

1) First you must build a _____ trap. It's best to build it out of

some _____ so that it's nice and _____. Once you

finish, give it a big _____ to make sure it will hold.

2) Next you need some bait. Like a/an _____, it prefers

_____ foods that are easy to _____. You may want to

try using _____ or _____.

3) Once your trap is set, hide behind a pile of _____ or in

some bushes.

4) Now you need to call to it. _____ your lips and give a loud whistle

like a/an _____. Repeat this until the creature comes to the trap.

5) Be careful when removing it from the trap, it could _____ you

with its _____ tail!

MAD LIBS JUNIOR™ is fun to play with friends, but you can also play it by yourself! To begin, look at the story on the page below. When you come to a blank space in the story, look at the symbol that appears underneath. Then find the same symbol on this page and pick a word that appears below the symbol. Put that word in the blank space, and cross out the word, so you don't use it again. Continue doing this throughout the story until you've filled in all the spaces. Finally, read your story aloud and laugh!

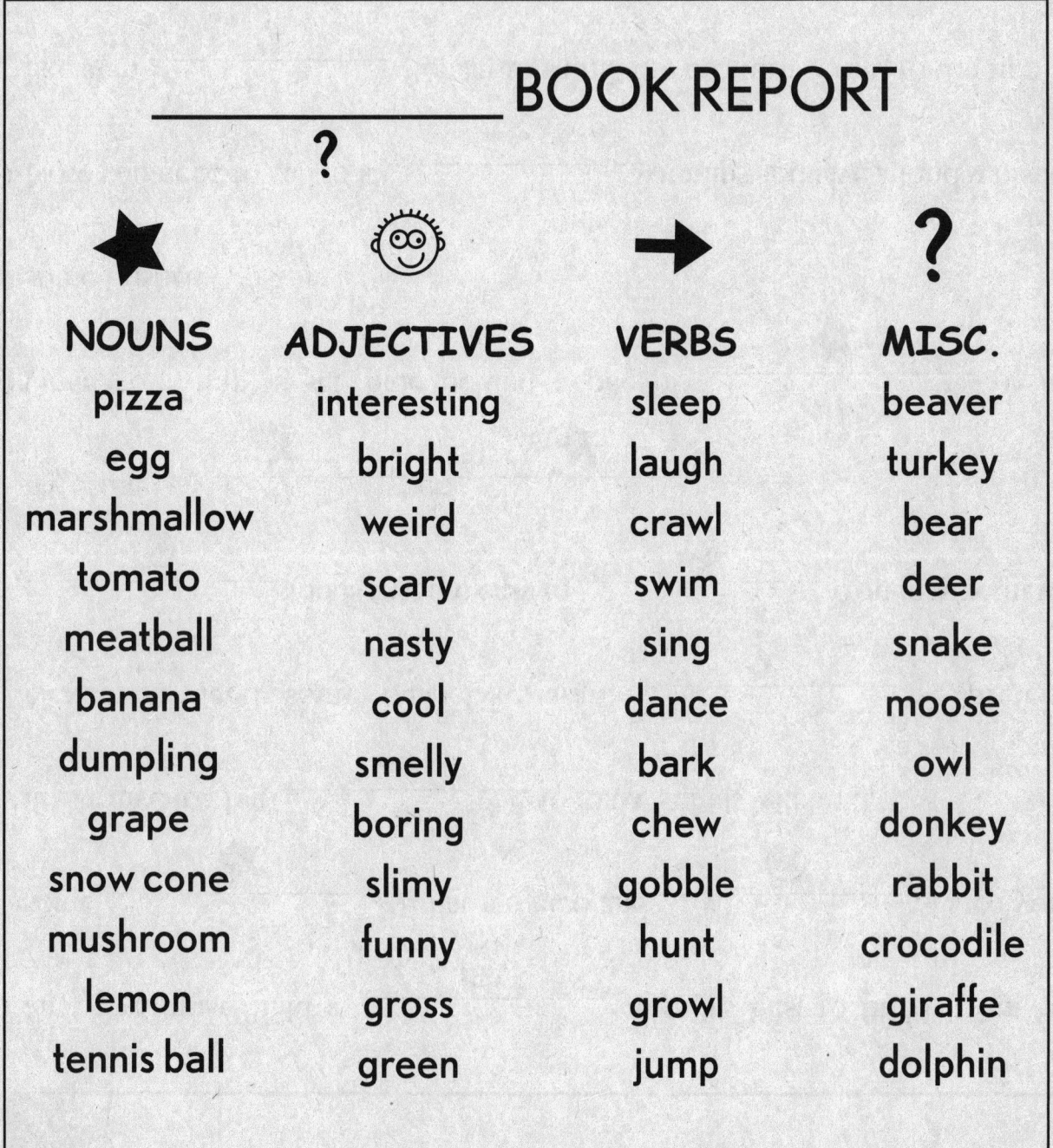

_____ BOOK REPORT
?

★ NOUNS	☺ ADJECTIVES	➡ VERBS	? MISC.
pizza	interesting	sleep	beaver
egg	bright	laugh	turkey
marshmallow	weird	crawl	bear
tomato	scary	swim	deer
meatball	nasty	sing	snake
banana	cool	dance	moose
dumpling	smelly	bark	owl
grape	boring	chew	donkey
snow cone	slimy	gobble	rabbit
mushroom	funny	hunt	crocodile
lemon	gross	growl	giraffe
tennis ball	green	jump	dolphin

MAD LIBS ✪ JUNIOR.
_____ BOOK REPORT
?

My teacher said we each had to do a book report about a/an

_____ _____, so I chose the turtle. A turtle has a hard
?

shell that's shaped like a/an _____. Its body inside the shell is

squishy like a/an _____. If the turtle comes across something

_____, it pulls its head and legs inside of its shell and starts to

_____. A turtle's favorite meal is a big _____

_____, but it will eat a/an _____ if it's really

hungry. Most people don't know that the turtle is related to the

_____ and that both of them _____

?

when they are attacked. My book report taught me that turtles are

really _____!

MAD LIBS JUNIOR™ is fun to play with friends, but you can also play it by yourself! To begin, look at the story on the page below. When you come to a blank space in the story, look at the symbol that appears underneath. Then find the same symbol on this page and pick a word that appears below the symbol. Put that word in the blank space, and cross out the word, so you don't use it again. Continue doing this throughout the story until you've filled in all the spaces. Finally, read your story aloud and laugh!

POLLY THE PARROT

★	😊	➡	?
NOUNS	**ADJECTIVES**	**VERBS**	**MISC.**
donut	crazy	clap	seal
gum ball	nervous	laugh	dog
hamburger	crunchy	sing	cat
olive	wacky	meow	llama
pumpkin	silly	talk	hippo
mirror	stupid	growl	shark
pickle	weird	bark	ostrich
flower	sick	dance	trout
light bulb	zany	cry	antelope
potato	kooky	shake	cheetah
pepper	wild	giggle	chicken
sweater	odd	cough	rat

My grandmother has a/an _____ 😊 parrot named Polly.

Whenever I visit, I always give Polly a little _____ ★ —they're her

favorite. Polly is such a/an _____ 😊 bird that every time the

phone rings, Polly starts to _____ ➡. And whenever you say,

"Hello, Polly," she says, "_____ ★ !" Her very favorite thing to say

is, "Polly wants a/an _____ ★ ." She sure is one _____ 😊

bird! One time she started chasing Grandma's pet _____ ?

around the kitchen. It was so scared that it started to _____ ➡ .

I don't think Polly even knows she's a parrot—she likes to

_____ ➡ just like a/an _____ 😊 _____ ? .

MAD LIBS JUNIOR™ is fun to play with friends, but you can also play it by yourself! To begin, look at the story on the page below. When you come to a blank space in the story, look at the symbol that appears underneath. Then find the same symbol on this page and pick a word that appears below the symbol. Put that word in the blank space, and cross out the word, so you don't use it again. Continue doing this throughout the story until you've filled in all the spaces. Finally, read your story aloud and laugh!

MY FAVORITE _____ MOVIE
?

★	☺	→	?
NOUNS	**ADJECTIVES**	**VERBS**	**MISC.**
apples	sick	yell	seal
pencils	wild	run	chipmunk
crackers	evil	jump	skunk
gumdrops	angry	cry	walrus
slippers	crazy	sing	lion
pickles	wacky	scream	badger
peaches	smelly	dance	hyena
pinecones	bashful	shake	canary
sugar cubes	stinky	growl	kangaroo
flowers	weird	bark	donkey
toothpicks	fuzzy	talk	dog
diamonds	chewy	laugh	rabbit

MAD LIBS JUNIOR
MY FAVORITE _____ MOVIE
?

My favorite _____ movie is about a _____ named

?

Mr. _____ who is good at solving crimes. His sidekick is a/an

★

_____ little _____ who likes to _____.

? ➡

The two of them have to stop a/an _____ _____ that has

?

stolen a bunch of _____ and is going to take over the world.

★

They follow a trail of _____ and chase him back to his

★

_____ lair. After a big chase scene, they catch him and he

starts to _____ like a/an _____ _____.

➡ **?**

They turn him in and are rewarded with a lifetime supply of

_____. What a/an _____ movie!

★

MAD LIBS JUNIOR™ is fun to play with friends, but you can also play it by yourself! To begin, look at the story on the page below. When you come to a blank space in the story, look at the symbol that appears underneath. Then find the same symbol on this page and pick a word that appears below the symbol. Put that word in the blank space, and cross out the word, so you don't use it again. Continue doing this throughout the story until you've filled in all the spaces. Finally, read your story aloud and laugh!

PET DAY

★	☺	➡	?
NOUNS	**ADJECTIVES**	**VERBS**	**MISC.**
pencils	furry	eat	turtle
carrots	slimy	bite	gorilla
erasers	exotic	sniff	goldfish
desks	smelly	lick	elephant
chairs	cool	grab	dinosaur
apples	fuzzy	kick	kangaroo
folders	bald	wiggle	dolphin
notebooks	weird	hug	shark
olives	crazy	shake	octopus
oranges	stinky	kiss	squirrel
spitballs	hairy	smell	tick
gum balls	wild	squeeze	antelope

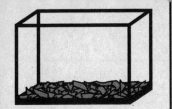

MAD LIBS JUNIOR
PET DAY

On pet day, everyone brought their _____ pets to school for

show-and-tell. My mom helped me pack my _____ **?** in a little

glass tank. Then we gave him a few _____ ★ to chew on during

the ride to school. When I got to school, everyone had brought a/an

_____ _____ **?**. My teacher even brought her

_____ pet _____ **?**. It liked to _____ ➡

_____ ★ and kept running around the classroom. Then Maria's

pet _____ **?** got loose and tried to _____ ➡ Jamie's pet

_____ **?**. Pet day was really _____, but I'm sure glad

it only happens once a year!

MAD LIBS JUNIOR™ is fun to play with friends, but you can also play it by yourself! To begin, look at the story on the page below. When you come to a blank space in the story, look at the symbol that appears underneath. Then find the same symbol on this page and pick a word that appears below the symbol. Put that word in the blank space, and cross out the word, so you don't use it again. Continue doing this throughout the story until you've filled in all the spaces. Finally, read your story aloud and laugh!

UNDERWATER ADVENTURE

★	☺	→	?
NOUNS	**ADJECTIVES**	**VERBS**	**MISC.**
pumpkin	fun	bite	manatee
hammer	slimy	kick	octopus
horseshoe	wet	swim	shark
noodle	cool	kiss	crab
pizza	nasty	hug	fish
pencil	squishy	sniff	clam
flower	awesome	lick	squid
hot dog	gross	grab	penguin
pretzel	boring	tickle	sea slug
star	wild	poke	stingray
pickle	wacky	pinch	walrus
clover	neat	rub	angelfish

MAD LIBS JUNIOR
UNDERWATER ADVENTURE

This summer, my family went on a/an _____ vacation to

Hawaii. One _____ day, we all went snorkeling. My sister

looked just like a/an _____ with her mask and fins on. Under

the water, we saw lots of _____ sea creatures. First we saw

a/an _____ that was shaped like a _____. Then

there was a/an _____ that was eating a _____. We

even saw a great white _____. It swam up so close that I

thought it might _____ me! But the very best part was when

a little _____ came up and started to _____

my dad right on the nose!

MAD LIBS JUNIOR™ is fun to play with friends, but you can also play it by yourself! To begin, look at the story on the page below. When you come to a blank space in the story, look at the symbol that appears underneath. Then find the same symbol on this page and pick a word that appears below the symbol. Put that word in the blank space, and cross out the word, so you don't use it again. Continue doing this throughout the story until you've filled in all the spaces. Finally, read your story aloud and laugh!

HOW TO CARE FOR A/AN _____ ?

★ NOUNS	😊 ADJECTIVES	➡ VERBS	? MISC.
lettuce	shiny	dance	jellyfish
onions	healthy	run	ferret
newspapers	clean	sing	snail
bubbles	slippery	hiccup	gerbil
orange juice	smelly	wiggle	hedgehog
vitamins	squishy	walk	hippo
apples	pretty	skip	octopus
snacks	fuzzy	jog	panda bear
candy	sturdy	play	zebra
lemons	soft	sneeze	rooster
tissues	rubbery	yell	gorilla
sugar cubes	nice	cough	hermit crab

MAD LIBS ⊕ JUNIOR

HOW TO CARE FOR A/AN _____ ?

1) Remember that they need lots of _____ ★ . Give them a fresh

bowlful every day.

2) Take your pet outside to _____ ➡ at least once a day. The

exercise and the air are good for a _____ ☺ coat.

3) Make sure your pet is living in a _____ ☺ tank or cage filled

with shredded _____ ★ that you change once a week.

4) Once a month, bathe your pet in some soapy water with some

_____ ★ added. This will make him extra _____ ☺ .

5) Anytime your pet starts to _____ ➡ in an odd way, be sure to

take him to the vet immediately.

MAD LIBS JUNIOR™ is fun to play with friends, but you can also play it by yourself! To begin, look at the story on the page below. When you come to a blank space in the story, look at the symbol that appears underneath. Then find the same symbol on this page and pick a word that appears below the symbol. Put that word in the blank space, and cross out the word, so you don't use it again. Continue doing this throughout the story until you've filled in all the spaces. Finally, read your story aloud and laugh!

PETTING ZOO

★	☺	➡	?
NOUNS	**ADJECTIVES**	**VERBS**	**MISC.**
jelly beans	best	bark	goats
cheese curls	worst	sniff	elephants
raisins	funniest	sweat	tigers
pretzels	smelliest	sing	anteaters
gum balls	coolest	cry	dinosaurs
seeds	silliest	grunt	horses
peanuts	craziest	dance	wombats
blueberries	wildest	snort	unicorns
olives	wackiest	growl	owls
potato chips	goofiest	cough	beavers
mints	stickiest	clap	crocodiles
popcorn	neatest	shake	mice

MAD LIBS JUNIOR
PETTING ZOO

Last week, our class went on the _____ field trip ever to the

petting zoo. This petting zoo had all kinds of _____—from

_____ to _____ and everything in between. For

twenty-five cents, you could buy a handful of _____ to feed to

the _____. They would _____ every time they

wanted a treat. The _____ kept trying to bite my clothes. I

think it's because I smell like _____. Some _____

ran up to my teacher, who got really scared and started to

_____. I laughed so hard that I began to _____.

That sure was the _____ petting zoo that I've ever been to!

MAD LIBS JUNIOR™ is fun to play with friends, but you can also play it by yourself! To begin, look at the story on the page below. When you come to a blank space in the story, look at the symbol that appears underneath. Then find the same symbol on this page and pick a word that appears below the symbol. Put that word in the blank space, and cross out the word, so you don't use it again. Continue doing this throughout the story until you've filled in all the spaces. Finally, read your story aloud and laugh!

THE CAMEL

★	☺	➡	?
NOUNS	**ADJECTIVES**	**VERBS**	**MISC.**
pineapples	hairy	eating	cheetah
bowling balls	gross	dancing	squirrel
sausages	weird	bathing	hippo
packages	fluffy	smooching	zebra
pizzas	strange	singing	llama
pillows	smelly	snorting	turtle
pumpkins	thirsty	yelling	antelope
cupcakes	lumpy	sneezing	mule
dumplings	crazy	drinking	giraffe
watermelons	silly	wiggling	porcupine
footballs	bumpy	laughing	polar bear
bags	furry	growling	horse

MAD LIBS JUNIOR
THE CAMEL

The camel is a very _____ _____. A camel looks kind of

like a big _____ with two _____ _____

stuck on its back. Camels live in the desert and can go for days without

_____. A camel can also run just like a/an _____,

and people can ride on its _____ back. Because they are so

_____, people often use them to carry _____ on

long trips across the desert. Just like the _____, camels are

known to have bad _____ habits. Camels also start

_____ when they get angry. So if you see an angry camel,

you'd better start _____!

From ANIMALS, ANIMALS, ANIMALS! MAD LIBS JUNIOR™ • Copyright © 2004 by
Penguin Random House LLC.

MAD LIBS JUNIOR™ is fun to play with friends, but you can also play it by yourself! To begin, look at the story on the page below. When you come to a blank space in the story, look at the symbol that appears underneath. Then find the same symbol on this page and pick a word that appears below the symbol. Put that word in the blank space, and cross out the word, so you don't use it again. Continue doing this throughout the story until you've filled in all the spaces. Finally, read your story aloud and laugh!

HATCHING BABIES

★	☺	→	?
NOUNS	**ADJECTIVES**	**VERBS**	**MISC.**
baseballs	slimy	shake	crocodiles
rocks	rubbery	wiggle	chickens
jelly beans	round	jump	snakes
gumdrops	fuzzy	giggle	dinosaurs
cotton balls	shiny	sing	lizards
grapes	scaly	yell	ducks
pearls	white	dance	turtles
golf balls	furry	bounce	owls
mushrooms	hairy	sneeze	butterflies
potatoes	slippery	move	frogs
marshmallows	cute	peep	ostriches
olives	weird	jiggle	fish

MAD LIBS JUNIOR.
HATCHING BABIES

For a class project, we hatched baby _____ in our classroom.
?

My teacher brought in twelve little eggs that looked like _____

_____. We kept the eggs in a big _____ machine
★

to keep them warm. My teacher said that in the wild, the mother would

make a nest out of _____ and sit on the eggs until they started
★

to _____. After a few weeks, some of our eggs started to
➡

_____. Then the babies that looked like _____
➡

_____ began to crawl out. I was so excited that I started to
?

_____! For our next class project, we're going to learn how
➡

_____ are made!
★

MAD LIBS JUNIOR™ is fun to play with friends, but you can also play it by yourself! To begin, look at the story on the page below. When you come to a blank space in the story, look at the symbol that appears underneath. Then find the same symbol on this page and pick a word that appears below the symbol. Put that word in the blank space, and cross out the word, so you don't use it again. Continue doing this throughout the story until you've filled in all the spaces. Finally, read your story aloud and laugh!

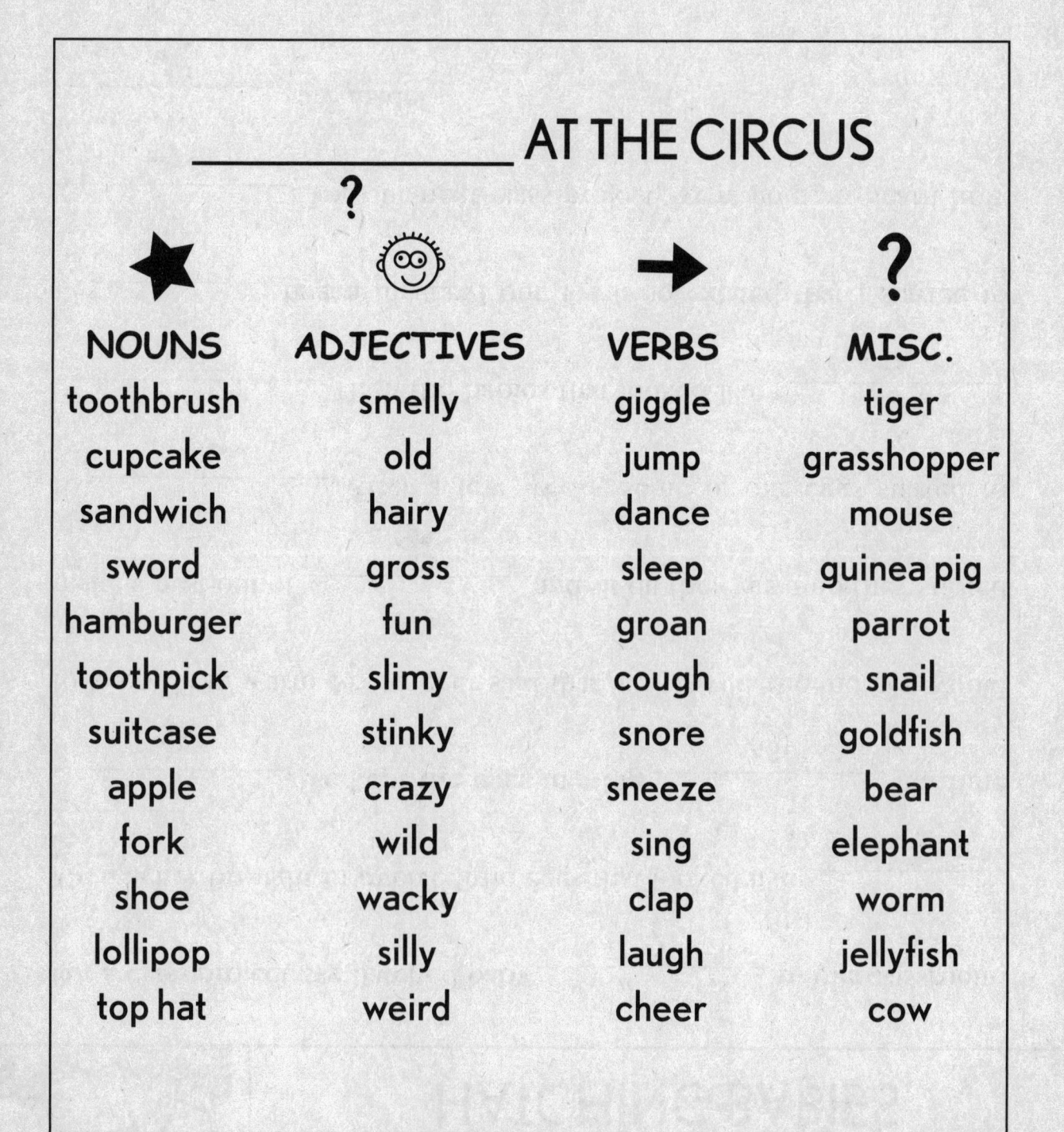

_____ AT THE CIRCUS
?

★ NOUNS	☺ ADJECTIVES	➡ VERBS	? MISC.
toothbrush	smelly	giggle	tiger
cupcake	old	jump	grasshopper
sandwich	hairy	dance	mouse
sword	gross	sleep	guinea pig
hamburger	fun	groan	parrot
toothpick	slimy	cough	snail
suitcase	stinky	snore	goldfish
apple	crazy	sneeze	bear
fork	wild	sing	elephant
shoe	wacky	clap	worm
lollipop	silly	laugh	jellyfish
top hat	weird	cheer	cow

MAD LIBS JUNIOR

_____ AT THE CIRCUS
?

On my birthday, my _____ Aunt Milly took me to the circus.

There was a/an _____ _____ there. There was a
?

lady in a/an _____ costume riding on the back of a/an

_____. Then a man in a/an _____ hat put his
?

_____ into a/an _____'s mouth. It was so scary
★ ?

that everyone in the audience started to _____. My favorite
→

_____ was a/an _____ that would _____
? ? →

every time his trainer said, "_____." My Aunt Milly said she
★

liked the _____ that swallowed a flaming _____
? ★

the best. Before we left, she bought me a big, stuffed _____.
?

The circus sure was _____!

MAD LIBS JUNIOR™ is fun to play with friends, but you can also play it by yourself! To begin, look at the story on the page below. When you come to a blank space in the story, look at the symbol that appears underneath. Then find the same symbol on this page and pick a word that appears below the symbol. Put that word in the blank space, and cross out the word, so you don't use it again. Continue doing this throughout the story until you've filled in all the spaces. Finally, read your story aloud and laugh!

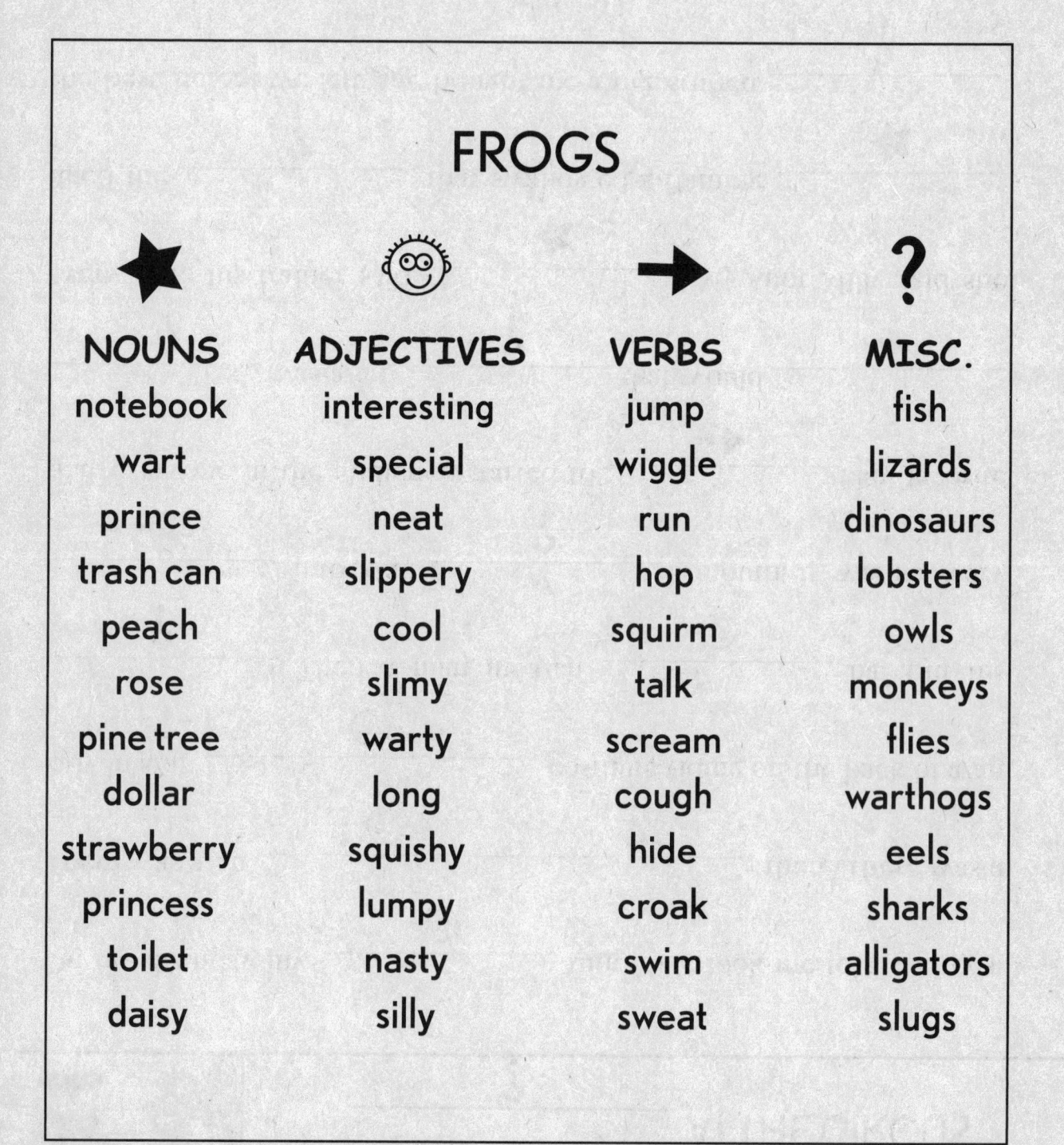

FROGS

★	☺	→	?
NOUNS	**ADJECTIVES**	**VERBS**	**MISC.**
notebook	interesting	jump	fish
wart	special	wiggle	lizards
prince	neat	run	dinosaurs
trash can	slippery	hop	lobsters
peach	cool	squirm	owls
rose	slimy	talk	monkeys
pine tree	warty	scream	flies
dollar	long	cough	warthogs
strawberry	squishy	hide	eels
princess	lumpy	croak	sharks
toilet	nasty	swim	alligators
daisy	silly	sweat	slugs

MAD LIBS JUNIOR
FROGS

Frogs are very _____ creatures. They start off as _____

little things called tadpoles. Tadpoles hatch from tiny _____-

looking eggs. They have tails like _____ and big eyes like

?

_____. After a little while, the tadpoles start to

?

_____ and grow arms and legs. Frogs can be hard to catch

➡

because they like to _____. One time I caught a big,

➡

_____ frog that smelled like a _____. I heard in a

★

fairy tale that if you kiss a frog, it will turn into a _____. But I

★

tried it and the frog just started to _____. Oh, well. Maybe I'll

➡

try kissing _____ instead!

?

MAD LIBS JUNIOR™ is fun to play with friends, but you can also play it by yourself! To begin, look at the story on the page below. When you come to a blank space in the story, look at the symbol that appears underneath. Then find the same symbol on this page and pick a word that appears below the symbol. Put that word in the blank space, and cross out the word, so you don't use it again. Continue doing this throughout the story until you've filled in all the spaces. Finally, read your story aloud and laugh!

HOW TO TEACH YOUR PET A TRICK

★ NOUNS	☺ ADJECTIVES	➡ VERBS	? MISC.
TV	slow	bark	lions
bone	quick	yell	poodles
scarf	dumb	sit	porcupines
CD	silly	sing	hermit crabs
computer	weird	sleep	wolves
steak	odd	whistle	aardvarks
cookie	fast	giggle	goldfish
sausage	crispy	cook	rats
trophy	lazy	sneeze	ladybugs
cupcake	wild	shake	newts
quarter	boring	growl	worms
candy bar	crazy	clap	mammoths

MAD LIBS JUNIOR
HOW TO TEACH YOUR PET A TRICK

1) Be patient. Some pets are _____, and some pets are

_____, and they all learn differently. (_____ and

_____ are very good at learning tricks.)

2) Give your pet a treat, like a _____ or a _____,

and say, "_____ girl or boy," every time your pet does a trick

correctly.

3) If you are trying to teach your pet to _____, show

your pet how it's done first.

4) Train your pet with a/an _____ command. For example,

you may want to _____ every time you want your pet to

_____.

5) Always remember to have fun with your _____ pet!

MAD LIBS JUNIOR™ is fun to play with friends, but you can also play it by yourself! To begin, look at the story on the page below. When you come to a blank space in the story, look at the symbol that appears underneath. Then find the same symbol on this page and pick a word that appears below the symbol. Put that word in the blank space, and cross out the word, so you don't use it again. Continue doing this throughout the story until you've filled in all the spaces. Finally, read your story aloud and laugh!

MY CAMPING TRIP

★	☺	→	?
NOUNS	**ADJECTIVES**	**VERBS**	**MISC.**
gum balls	silly	singing	mouse
pinecones	crazy	snoring	lion
cabbage	wacky	sneezing	moose
hot dogs	funny	whistling	snake
marshmallows	stinky	growling	dinosaur
mushrooms	goofy	barking	owl
sticks	scary	laughing	tiger
eggs	wild	screaming	porcupine
coconuts	kooky	talking	wolf
noodles	weird	howling	grizzly bear
ice cream	smelly	giggling	anteater
apples	strange	coughing	shark

My _____ family went on a camping trip to the mountains. At

night we made a big campfire and roasted _____ ★ for dinner.

When I went to bed in my tent, I could hear a wild _____ ?

_____ → in the woods. I heard something _____ → right

near my _____ tent. I peeked out and saw a big

_____ ? eating some _____! ★ It heard me

_____ → and ran off into the woods. Then I felt something on

my foot and I was so scared, I started _____. → My mom came

running, but it was only a little _____ ? that had gotten into my

tent. What a _____ adventure!

MAD LIBS JUNIOR™ is fun to play with friends, but you can also play it by yourself! To begin, look at the story on the page below. When you come to a blank space in the story, look at the symbol that appears underneath. Then find the same symbol on this page and pick a word that appears below the symbol. Put that word in the blank space, and cross out the word, so you don't use it again. Continue doing this throughout the story until you've filled in all the spaces. Finally, read your story aloud and laugh!

BREAKING NEWS

★	☺	→	?
NOUNS	**ADJECTIVES**	**VERBS**	**MISC.**
crackers	crazy	attack	turtle
pets	angry	read	goat
meatballs	sleepy	run	octopus
gumdrops	mad	talk	zebra
pickles	confused	dance	tiger
carrots	happy	move	hippo
vegetables	dizzy	giggle	bear
noodles	tired	sing	seal
snacks	grumpy	jump	reindeer
hot dogs	sick	faint	camel
flowers	wild	sneeze	python
bicycles	silly	laugh	weasel

MAD LIBS JUNIOR
BREAKING NEWS

"Attention, everyone. This is your _____ newscaster. We have

breaking news to report on. While its cage was being cleaned, a/an

_____ _____ ? escaped from the city zoo this

morning. Zookeepers say the _____ ? is _____ and

_____ and you should not try to catch it yourself. It's about

the size of a/an _____ ? and it likes to _____ → and

will eat any _____ ★ it comes in contact with. If you have any

_____ ★ outside in your yard, you are urged to bring them

inside. If you see this _____ ? near your home, try not to

_____ → . Sudden movements might make the _____ ?

feel _____ , and it could _____ → . Call the zoo hotline

at 1-800-_____ _____ ? if you see anything."

MAD LIBS JUNIOR™ is fun to play with friends, but you can also play it by yourself! To begin, look at the story on the page below. When you come to a blank space in the story, look at the symbol that appears underneath. Then find the same symbol on this page and pick a word that appears below the symbol. Put that word in the blank space, and cross out the word, so you don't use it again. Continue doing this throughout the story until you've filled in all the spaces. Finally, read your story aloud and laugh!

BUTTERFLIES

★ NOUNS	😊 ADJECTIVES	→ VERBS	? MISC.
leaves	interesting	swim	elephant
flowers	crazy	dance	caterpillar
socks	strange	sing	sparrow
hats	slimy	laugh	turtle
elves	cool	eat	ostrich
acorns	fuzzy	play	sloth
mushrooms	boring	hide	kangaroo
lollipops	pretty	hunt	porcupine
cupcakes	weird	fly	jellyfish
plants	awesome	roam	snake
fairies	smart	live	pony
pickles	wacky	shop	octopus

I like to watch _____ nature shows on TV. The other night,

I saw one about butterflies. Butterflies are really _____

creatures. The butterfly starts off as an egg that hatches into a/an

_____ **?** . It eats lots of _____ ★ , then spins a/an

_____ case around itself called a cocoon. After several days,

the _____ butterfly comes out of the cocoon. Butterflies like

to _____ ➡ in the wild and they can have many different kinds

of wings. Some butterflies even look like _____ ★ . That way, if

an enemy like a/an _____ **?** comes along in the wild, it won't

try to eat the butterfly. Nature sure is _____ !

Join the millions of Mad Libs fans creating wacky and wonderful stories on our apps!

Download Mad Libs today!